The

"How to Make Ketchup"

Cookbook

FAVORITE KETCHUP RECIPES FROM PICKLE JAR RANCH

BY

CRISI COOPER

Disclaimer
This book contains recipes that, regardless of my own results and experience, may not produce the same results (or any results) for you. I make absolutely no guarantees, expressed or implied. As with any endeavor, you assume all risk.

First Printing, 2012
Printed in the United States of America

ISBN-13: 978-1478211532
ISBN-10: 1478211539

This book was published with the assistance of the great folks at
BookroomPublishing.com

Acknowledgements

I would like to thank all the children of Pickle Jar Ranch for inspiring me to cook new things and being willing to try them when I do...

In order of their appearance, they are:
Madison
Aubrey
Aislyn
Isabella
Anna
Ellaina
Colin
And the little girl who is still cooking...

I love you guys.

P.S. Thanks for giving me a turn in the wagon too!

Table of Contents

Introduction

Here at Pickle Jar Ranch, the foray into the world of ketchup-making all began when we ran out. Obviously, you cannot be without ketchup if you have six grandchildren at the house for the weekend. We had a beautiful kitchen garden overflowing with tomatoes, so I decided to make home-made ketchup. Sounds simple, right? Maybe not so much...

I started by calling my mother and asking if she had a recipe. She didn't, she'd never made ketchup. She referred me to an old canning book. I tried the recipe I found there. It was good. Not great, but good. And it was worthy of further investigation because I had glimpsed something wonderful glimmering in the distance.

Intrigued, I asked some of my cooking friends if they had a recipe for ketchup. I got several responses, and when I saw a recipe using fruit, my understanding of 'ketchup' was changed forever.

After some additional research, I found that ketchup was originally a thin sauce like soy or Worcestershire sauce.

We aren't making sauces like that in these recipes. We are making ketchup about the thickness of traditional 'store-bought' tomato ketchup, but we *are* going to be making it in many different flavors.

There is some controversy over whether it is 'catsup' or 'ketchup'. I chose to use 'ketchup', a choice that is due entirely to the fact that I didn't want to use the phrase "Crisi Cooper's Catsup Cookbook"...

Regardless, I am now on the ketchup bandwagon. I can easily imagine that there is a flavor of ketchup appropriate for every occasion.

Grape Ketchup? Really? Turns out, it's crazy good with lamb. Which kind of makes sense when you think about it. Banana Lime Ketchup? Amazing with grilled pork chops and simply incredible with sweet-potato fries. Green Tomato Ketchup? It's sassy and I'm on board!

The fact that you are reading this means that you realize, or at least suspect, that there is more to this much-maligned condiment than first believed. It means that you have stopped thinking about ketchup as just that tomato-y stuff for fries, and have begun envisioning ketchup as a sauce, a glorious bouquet of flavors brought together to enhance your meal and pleasure your taste buds.

These are not recipes for a gourmet chef, filled with masterful chef-ly technique, but are recipes intended for typical cooks in ordinary kitchens. All of the ingredients are readily available at your local grocery store. And you should have, or have easy access to, all the cooking utensils you need.

Some of these ketchups are intended for immediate, or near immediate, consumption. Others recipes call for 'canning' to help you preserve their luscious goodness for months, or even years. Don't be afraid of the recipes that call for canning. Canning tomatoes, and almost any high acid fruit product, is something that even an inexperienced cook can manage just by following a few basic directions. But if you decide not to 'can', most of these ketchups will keep in the fridge for about a month or so.

These recipes can be halved without adverse effect, which is nice if you only want a small amount. Equally, you can double the recipes for your favorites.

Due to the vagaries of the fruit used in canning, as well as the particular mood of the cook on any given day, each time we make a batch it is slightly different from any we've made before. That's a good thing, I think. You should feel free to add a dash of something of your own here and there as you go through a cookbook. That's the pleasure of being the cook.

I am interested in hearing how you are making each recipe your own, so e-mail me at: **KetchupCook@gmail.com**

Until then, so long from the Pickle Jar Ranch.

Crisi
(aka 'Mee-Maw')

An Antique Recipe

Get [the tomatoes] quite ripe on a dry day, squeeze them with your hands till reduced to a pulp, then put half a pound of fine salt to one hundred tomatoes, and boil them for two hours.

Stir them to prevent burning.

While hot, press them through a fine sieve with a silver spoon till nought but the skin remains, then add a little mace, 3 nutmegs, allspice, cloves, cinnamon, ginger, and pepper to taste.

Boil over a slow fire till quite thick, stir all the time.

Bottle when cold.

One hundred tomatoes will make four or five bottles and keep good for two or three years.

Sandy Addison, Sugar House Book, 1801

Sweet Tomato Ketchup

This is a tried and true recipe. I keep this on hand at all times. It's probably the closest thing to 'traditional' ketchup that you will find at PJR.

This recipe calls for 'canning' the sauce to preserve it, so be sure to see the **Notes About Canning** at the end of the book.

Ingredients:

8 pounds ripe tomatoes*
1 medium onion, chopped
1 small green bell pepper, chopped
1/4 teaspoon cayenne pepper
1/4 teaspoon black pepper

3/4 cup sugar
1/4 cup brown sugar

3/4 cup apple cider vinegar
1/4 cup apple juice
2 cloves of garlic, crushed
1/2 teaspoon allspice
1/2 teaspoon dry mustard
1-1/2 teaspoon whole cloves
1 piece cinnamon stick, broken
1 teaspoon celery seed

4 teaspoons salt

1 can tomato paste, 6 oz. (optional)

* You can substitute canned crushed tomatoes in this recipe. See my **Notes** on page 54.

Preparation:

Start by washing the fruit. Some people like to peel their tomatoes before chopping and cooking them. I think this just adds another step because I am going to run the sauce through a colander later. But if you prefer, you can peel tomatoes by dipping them, a few at a time, into boiling water for a minute or two. Use a ladle or long-handled slotted spoon to retrieve them, and then plunge them into icy cold water. The skin will slip off with a little help from a knife. Be careful, they are HOT!

If you are not peeling the tomatoes, quarter them and remove the stem ends, tough cores and any significant blemishes.

Wash, de-seed and de-stem the bell pepper. Chop coarsely.

Peel and coarsely chop the onions.

Combine the tomatoes, onion, and bell pepper in a large, non-reactive pot (stainless or enameled). Simmer until tender, about 20 to 30 minutes, stirring occasionally to prevent sticking.

Working in batches, carefully puree the mixture in a blender, food processor, or with an emersion blender.

If using a blender:
Don't overfill the blender. Be careful when you are processing the sauce because the hot steam can sometimes blow the lid off. (Guess how we figured that out!)

Start the blender on a low speed with the lid slightly open on one side to vent any steam, then gradually seal the lid and increase the blending speed.

Transfer the mixture to a sieve or colander placed over a glass or stainless steel bowl and press with the back of a spoon to extract all the liquid and pulp. You can also do this in a food mill. You are trying to process as much of the essence of the tomato as possible, leaving behind only a dry-ish pulp of seed (and skins if you haven't already peeled them.)

Rinse the pot (or use a fresh pot) and refill with the strained tomato puree. Start over a medium heat. Add the cayenne and black pepper, and sugars to the tomato sauce, stirring in thoroughly.

Note the depth of the sauce on your spoon. Bring to a boil, uncovered. Reduce heat slightly and simmer briskly 1-1/2 to 2 hours or until sauce is reduced by about half, stirring occasionally to prevent sticking.

Meanwhile, in a small saucepan combine the rest of the ingredients, except the salt. Bring the vinegar and spice mixture to a boil. Reduce heat, cover, and simmer for 15 minutes, stirring occasionally. Remove from heat. Let the vinegar and spices stand while sauce is reducing.

When the sauce is reduced to about half, about an hour, strain spiced vinegar mixture into tomato sauce. Discard the coarse spice parts that were strained out. Add salt to the sauce, adjusting the amount to taste.

Stirring frequently, simmer until the ketchup reaches desired consistency, about 30 minutes to an hour.

Typically, I will also add a small (6 oz.) can of tomatoe paste to hasten the thickening process.

When the sauce is of the desired consistency, pour/ladle hot ketchup into hot jars, (a wide-mouthed funnel is very helpful) leaving 1/2 inch headspace. Wipe rim of jar. Seal with new, pre-simmered lids, and screw down rings firmly.

For pint jars, process:

15 minutes at 0-1000 ft.
20 minutes at 1001- 6000 ft. and
25 minutes above 6000 ft.

Use 5 minutes less for half pints.

Best if left to mature for 2 weeks before using.

Yield: 4-5 pints

The Pickle Jar Ranch logo is a cartoon drawing of our very first goat, Dink. It was drawn by Kenneth M. Lively.

Quick Tomato Ketchup

Sometimes you need ketchup in a hurry. If that's the case, this is your recipe. It is best if you can let this set overnight in order for the flavors to ripen, but it's really pretty good as soon as it's made.

Ingredients:

4 pounds ripe tomatoes, coarsely chopped*
1-1/2 cups granulated sugar
1 cup apple cider vinegar
1 clove garlic, finely chopped and crushed
3/4 teaspoon salt
1 1/2 teaspoon pickling spices
1/4 stick cinnamon
1-1/2 teaspoon dry mustard
1/4 to 1/2 teaspoon freshly ground pepper
1/4 teaspoon cayenne pepper

2 tablespoon cornstarch
1/4 cup cold water

* You can substitute canned crushed tomatoes in this recipe. See my **Notes** on page 54.

Preparation:

Always begin by washing your produce. Quarter and remove the stem ends, tough cores, and any significant blemishes on the tomatoes.

Combine everything but the cornstarch and water in a large, non-reactive pot. Bring to a boil over a medium heat, stirring occasionally to prevent sticking. Reduce the heat and simmer uncovered for about 30 minutes, stirring frequently. Remove from heat.

Working in batches, carefully puree the mixture in a blender, food processor, or with an emersion blender.

If using a blender:
Don't overfill the blender. Be careful when you are processing the sauce because the hot steam can sometimes blow the lid off. (Guess how we figured that out!)

Start the blender on a low speed with the lid slightly open on one side to vent any steam, then gradually seal the lid and increase the blending speed.

Transfer the mixture to a sieve or colander placed over a glass or stainless steel bowl and press with the back of a spoon to extract all the liquid and pulp. You can also do this in a food mill. You are trying to process as much of the essence of the tomatoe as possible, leaving behind only a dry-ish pulp of seed and skin.

Rinse the pot (or use a fresh pot) and refill with the strained tomato puree. Start over a medium heat and bring to a boil, stirring occasionally to prevent sticking.

Mix the cornstarch and cold water together thoroughly, and then add to the simmering tomato mixture.

Return the ketchup to a boil over medium heat, stirring frequently. Simmer the ketchup, stirring frequently, for 10 minutes. Even if the ketchup seems thin, do not cook it any longer. (Cook it for more than 10 minutes and instead of the sauce thicker getting thicker, it will actually start to thin).

The ketchup will thicken a bit as it cools. Remove the ketchup from the heat and let it cool to room temperature. Store in the refrigerator in a reseal-able container or jar for up to one month.

Yield: about 5 cups (2-1/2 pints)

Spicy Roasted Ketchup

We use this ketchup when making red beans and rice, and as a marinade before grilling chicken.

This recipe calls for 'canning' the sauce to preserve it, so be sure to see the **Notes About Canning** at the end of the book. If you don't 'can' the ketchup, you can keep it your fridge for up to a month.

Ingredients:

6 pounds ripe tomatoes*
2 chili peppers (green or red)
2 jalapeno peppers
3-4 tablespoons olive oil

1 large onion, chopped
2 large cloves garlic, chopped and crushed

1/4 teaspoon cayenne pepper
1/4 teaspoon black pepper
1/2 teaspoon crushed red pepper
1 teaspoon chili powder
1 tablespoon Worcestershire sauce

1/3 cup honey
1/3 cup granulated sugar
1/3 cup molasses

1 cup apple cider vinegar
1/4 teaspoon allspice
1/2 teaspoon dry mustard
1 1/2 teaspoon whole cloves
1 piece cinnamon stick, broken
1 teaspoon celery seed
1 teaspoon smoked paprika
4 teaspoon sea salt

1-6 oz. can tomato paste (optional)

Preparation:

Preheat oven or grill to 450 degrees.

Wash the tomatoes. Quarter and remove the stem ends, tough cores, and any significant blemishes.

Clean, de-seed, and chop the chili and jalapeño peppers.

Spread the tomatoes and peppers evenly over two cookie sheets, cut side up, and drizzle very lightly with olive oil. Roast for about 20 minutes, or until slightly browned and wrinkled, but not burned.

Meanwhile, in a large non-reactive (stainless or enameled) stock pot, sauté onions and garlic in olive oil until onions are translucent.

In a large stockpot, combine the roasted tomatoes and peppers, onion, garlic, cayenne, black and crushed red pepper, chili powder, and Worcestershire sauce. Simmer mixture about 15 minutes, until everything is tender, stirring occasionally to prevent sticking.

Working in batches, carefully puree the mixture in a blender, food processor, or with an emersion blender.

If using a blender:
Don't overfill the blender. Be careful when you are processing the sauce because the hot steam can sometimes blow the lid off. (Guess how we figured that out!)

Start the blender on a low speed with the lid slightly open on one side to vent any steam, then gradually seal the lid and increase the blending speed.

Transfer the blended mixture to a sieve or colander placed over a glass or stainless steel bowl and press with the back of a spoon to extract all the liquid and pulp. You can also do this in a food mill. You are trying to process as much of the essence of the tomatoe as possible, leaving behind only a dry-ish pulp of seed and skin.

Rinse the pot (or use a fresh pot) and refill with the strained tomatoe/pepper puree. Return to medium heat.

Add the honey, granulated sugar, and molasses to tomato mixture, stirring in thoroughly. Note the depth of the sauce on your spoon.

Bring to a boil; then simmer briskly 1 1/2 to 2 hours or until sauce is reduced by about half, stirring occasionally to prevent sticking.

Meanwhile, in small saucepan combine: apple cider vinegar, allspice, dry mustard, whole cloves, cinnamon stick, and celery seed. Bring the mixture to a boil. Reduce heat, cover, and simmer for 30 minutes, stirring occasionally. Remove from heat. Let stand while sauce is reducing.

When the sauce is reduced by about half, strain the spiced vinegar mixture into tomato sauce, then discard the coarse bits strained from the spices. Stir the sea salt into the mixture.

Stirring frequently, simmer until sauce reaches desired consistency, about 30 minutes to 1 hour. Typically, we will add a small (6 oz.) can of tomatoe paste to hasten the thickening process.

Pour/ladle hot ketchup into hot jars, (a wide-mouthed funnel is very helpful) leaving 1/2 inch headspace. Wipe rim of jar. Seal with new, pre-simmered lids, and screw down rings firmly.

For pint jars, process:

15 minutes at 0-1000 ft.
20 minutes at 1001- 6000 ft. and
25 minutes above 6000 ft.

Use 5 minutes less for half pints.

The ketchup, like most canned goods, tastes best if left to stand for 2 weeks before using, allowing the flavors to meld and mature.

Yield: 4-5 pints

Dink came to the family as a tiny, starved, mixed-breed rescue. It took a while, but he eventually grew into the magnificently-horned guardian of our herd.

Curry Ketchup

My brother tells me that this is an authentic German recipe. I don't know about that, but if you are looking for a chunky sauce to serve with big wedges of fried potatoes or with a bratwurst hotdog, this is just the ticket. Quick and easy!

Ingredients:

1 bunch of tender green onions, finely chopped
1 clove garlic, chopped and crushed
1 teaspoon ginger

1 can crushed tomatoes, 28-ounce*
¼ - ½ teaspoon curry powder (to taste)
1/2 teaspoon ground turmeric

Salt and pepper (to taste)
Splash of Worcestershire sauce (to taste)

Preparation:

*You can also use 1-1/2 pounds of fresh garden tomatoes (five to six medium to large tomatoes). They will need to be peeled. Peel tomatoes by dipping them, a few at a time, into boiling water for a minute or two. Use a ladle or long-handled slotted spoon to retrieve them, and then plunge them into icy cold water. The skin will slip off with a little help from a knife. De-stemmed and chop coarsely. Be careful, they are HOT!

In a saucepan, simmer the onions, garlic, and ginger with just enough water to keep them from sticking until the onions are tender (4 or 5 minutes).

Add the tomatoes, curry powder, and turmeric. Mix well.

Add salt, pepper, and Worcestershire sauce to taste. Cook for another 30 minutes to blend flavors. Serve hot.

Yield: 1-2 pints

Dink is something of a celebrity at PJR because of his ability to eat large quantities of jalapenos. He can also leap tall fences in a single bound.

Green Tomato Ketchup

This is an old recipe using green tomatoes that has a really nice flavor! The kids use this ketchup on fries and burgers just like red ketchup. I've been meaning to try using banana instead of poblano chili peppers for something a little milder...

I don't run this through a sieve, preferring the coarse texture of this heated condiment.

This recipe calls for 'canning' the sauce to preserve it, so be sure to see the **Notes About Canning** at the end of the book.

Ingredients:

5 pounds green tomatoes
5 poblano peppers
3 medium-sized onions, chopped
3 tablespoon salt

3 cups apple cider vinegar
1/2 tablespoon powdered ginger
1/2 tablespoon ground cloves
1 tablespoon dry mustard
1/2 teaspoon nutmeg

1 cup sugar
Salt and pepper to taste, about a teaspoon of each

Preparation:

Begin by washing the produce. Remove any significant blemishes on the tomatoes, and then chop coarsely.

De-seed, de-core, and coarsely chop the peppers.

Coarsely chop the onions.

Combine the tomatoes, peppers, and onions in a large pot or bowl, sprinkling the mixture lightly with salt. Mix well, cover, and let set for at least four hours (or even overnight) in the refrigerator.

Drain off the liquid and combine the tomato/onion mixture in a large stock pot with the vinegar, ginger, cloves, mustard, and nutmeg.

Simmer until tender, about 30-45 minutes, stirring occasionally to prevent sticking.

Working in batches, carefully puree the tomato/onion mixture in a blender, food processor, or with an emersion blender.

If using a blender:
Don't overfill the blender. Be careful when you are processing the sauce because the hot steam can sometimes blow the lid off. (Guess how we figured that out!)

Start the blender on a low speed with the lid slightly open on one side to vent any steam, then gradually seal the lid and increase the blending speed.

Return the puree to a clean pot. Add the sugar, then salt and pepper to taste. Bring to a boil, then reduce heat and simmer very slowly, uncovered, for 45 minutes, adding a little vinegar if the ketchup starts to look too thick.

Pour/ladle hot ketchup into hot jars, (a wide-mouthed funnel is very helpful) leaving 1/2 inch headspace. Wipe rim of jar. Seal with new, pre-simmered lids, and screw down rings firmly.

For pint jars, process:

15 minutes at 0-1000 ft.
20 minutes at 1001- 6000 ft. and
25 minutes above 6000 ft.

Use 5 minutes less for half pints.

Best if left to stand for 2 weeks before using.

Yield: 3-4 pints

Peppery Tomato Ketchup

Maybe it's because we're Texans, but we sometimes like a little kick in our ketchup. I use this as part of my chili base. This is straight forward, no-frills peppery ketchup.

This recipe calls for 'canning' the sauce to preserve it, so be sure to see the **Notes About Canning** at the end of the book.

If you don't 'can' the ketchup, you can keep it in your fridge for up to a month.

Ingredients:

6 pounds ripe tomatoes*
1 cup jalapeno peppers (about 6)
1 cup green or red chili peppers (about 6)
2 medium onions
4 cloves garlic
2 stalks celery

2 cups apple cider vinegar
3/4 cup brown sugar
2-4 teaspoon salt

1-6 oz. can tomato paste (optional)

Preparation:

* You can substitute canned crushed tomatoes in this recipe. See my **Notes** on page 54.

Wash the tomatoes. Quarter and remove the stem ends, tough cores, and any significant blemishes. Clean, de-seed, and coarsely chop the peppers. Clean and chop the onions. Clean, chop, and crush the garlic. Finely chop the celery.

Combine the tomatoes, peppers, onion, garlic and celery in a large, non-reactive pot (stainless or enameled). Simmer about 20-30 minutes, until the celery is are tender, stirring occasionally to prevent sticking.

Working in batches, carefully puree the mixture in a blender, food processor, or with an emersion blender.

If using a blender:
Don't overfill the blender. Be careful when you are processing the sauce because the hot steam can sometimes blow the lid off. (Guess how we figured that out!)

Start the blender on a low speed with the lid slightly open on one side to vent any steam, then gradually seal the lid and increase the blending speed.

Transfer the mixture to a sieve or colander placed over a glass or stainless steel bowl and press with the back of a spoon to extract all the liquid and pulp. You can also do this in a food mill.

Return the mixture to a clean pot. Add the sugar and spices to the tomato/pepper sauce.

Stirring frequently to prevent sticking, simmer until sauce reaches desired consistency, about 1-1/2 to 2 hours. You may add a small (6 oz.) can of tomato paste to hasten the thickening process.

Pour/ladle hot ketchup into hot jars, (a wide-mouthed canning funnel is very helpful) leaving 1/2 inch headspace. Wipe rim. Seal with new, pre-simmered lids, and screw down rings firmly.

For pint jars, process:
15 minutes at 0-1000 ft.
20 minutes at 1001- 6000 ft. and
25 minutes above 6000 ft.

Use 5 minutes less for half pints.

Best if left to stand for 2 weeks before using.

Yield: 4-5 pints

Ancho Chili Ketchup

Wow! When my friend Dee gave me this recipe, I immediately knew that we were going to love it! Ancho chili are sweet, with a wonderful warm flavor, and this ketchup is fantastic with grilled chicken and fish.

This recipe calls for 'canning' the sauce to preserve it, so be sure to see the **Notes About Canning** at the end of the book.

If you don't 'can' the ketchup, you can keep it your fridge for up to a month.

Ingredients:

12 Ancho chili peppers
1 medium onion, finely chopped
5 cloves garlic, chopped and crushed
6 cups water

5 teaspoons brown sugar
2 tablespoons ground cumin
1 teaspoon apple cider vinegar (or a good splash)
1 tablespoon lime juice
2- 6 oz. cans tomato paste

Salt to taste, about 1/2 teaspoon
Freshly ground pepper to taste, about 1/2 teaspoon

Preparation:

De-stem, de-seed, and coarsely chop the Ancho peppers.

Combine the peppers, onion, garlic, and water in a saucepan. Bring the mixture to a boil, then reduce heat and simmer for about 15 minutes. (You need the peppers to absorb some water and to soften.)

Strain the peppers, onion, and garlic. (Keep the pepper water to use later in the recipe*). Then combine the strained products with the brown sugar, cumin, tomato paste, vinegar, lime juice, and 1 cup of the pepper water.

Working in batches, carefully puree the spiced mixture in a blender, food processor, or with an emersion blender, adding more pepper water as needed to reach the desired consistency.

If using a blender:
Don't overfill the blender. Be careful when you are processing the sauce because the hot steam can sometimes blow the lid off. (Guess how we figured that out!)

Start the blender on a low speed with the lid slightly open on one side to vent any steam, then gradually seal the lid and increase the blending speed.

Return the mixture to a clean pot. Stirring frequently to prevent sticking, simmer until sauce reaches desired consistency, about 30 minutes, adding salt and pepper to taste.

If the sauce gets too thick, add pepper water.

Pour/ladle hot ketchup into hot jars, (a wide-mouthed canning funnel is very helpful) leaving 1/2 inch headspace. Wipe rim. Seal with new, pre-simmered lids, and screw down rings firmly.

For pint jars, process:

15 minutes at 0-1000 ft.
20 minutes at 1001- 6000 ft. and
25 minutes above 6000 ft.

Use 5 minutes less for half pints.

Best if left to stand for 2 weeks before using.

Yield: about 2-3 pints

**I also keep any unused pepper water for use in other dishes, storing it in a tightly covered container in the fridge for a week or more.*

Apple Pecan Ketchup

Because we live in the south, I have to include pecans in at least one recipe. This is really more of an apple nut relish, but it's truly delicious!

I don't remember where the recipe came from, but I always make sure I have some around on Thanksgiving because we love it with turkey sandwiches.

Ingredients

3 pounds tart green apples
2 large onions, chopped
1 banana (or other mild flavored) pepper, chopped
3-1/2 cups cider vinegar
1-3/4 cup brown sugar
1/2 cup corn syrup
1/3 cup molasses
1 teaspoon ground white pepper
1 teaspoon ground ginger
1/2 teaspoon allspice
1/2 teaspoon cinnamon
1/2 teaspoon clove
1/2 teaspoon coriander
1/2 teaspoon ginger and
1/2 teaspoon nutmeg

2 cups fresh pecans, chopped

Preparation

Peel, core, and remove any significant blemishes on the apples, then chop coarsely.

Coarsely chop the onions.

De-seed and de-stem the pepper. Chop coarsely.

Place the chopped apples in a large pot, along with all of the other ingredients except the pecans.

Bring to a boil, then reduce heat and simmer until apples are tender and the sauce begins to thicken (about 45 minutes).

Add the pecans, stirring it in thoroughly. Simmer another 5-10 minutes to thicken.

Pour/ladle hot ketchup into hot jars, (a wide-mouthed funnel is very helpful) leaving 1/2 inch headspace. Wipe rim of jar. Seal with new, pre-simmered lids, and screw down rings firmly.

For pint jars, process:

15 minutes at 0-1000 ft.
20 minutes at 1001- 6000 ft. and
25 minutes above 6000 ft.

Use 5 minutes less for half pints.

You can also store the ketchup in the refrigerator until ready to use. This will keep about a month.

Yield: 3-4 pints, depending on your fruit

Banana Lime Ketchup

It sounds weird, but this ketchup is the perfect blend of banana sweetness and lime tartness. It's amazing with grilled pork chops and sweet potato home fries.

One of my granddaughters also mixes it with mayo, making her own sauce for sweet potato fries (I think I see another cook in the family!)

Ingredients:

1 pound ripe bananas (about 2)
1/2 of a sweet purple onion
1/2 of a green chili pepper
2 cloves garlic
1-2 tablespoon EV olive oil

1/2 cup orange juice (or the juice from 1 large orange)
1-1/2 tablespoons light brown sugar
1/4 teaspoon ground cinnamon
1/4 teaspoon ground cloves
1 teaspoon paprika
1/2 teaspoon salt
1/4 teaspoon ground white pepper

1 tablespoon cider vinegar
1/3 cup lime juice

Preparation:

Peel and chop the bananas. Finely chop the onion. Chop and crush the garlic. De-seed and de-stem the chili pepper, then chop finely.

Combine the orange juice, brown sugar, cinnamon, cloves, salt and pepper in a small bowl and have ready to use. Have the vinegar and lime pre-measured as well. (Once the bananas start cooking, things go very quickly in this recipe!)

Heat the oil, and then add the onions and pepper. Sauté over medium heat until the onions are translucent. When the onions are almost ready, add the garlic (to keep the garlic from scorching). Add more oil if needed.

When the onions are translucent, reduce the heat to low. Allow the pan to cool somewhat before adding the bananas.

Cook the bananas about 2-4 minutes, stirring frequently to prevent sticking. Mash the bananas slightly as you cook them and keep them moving in the pan so they do not stick.

When the mixture becomes pasty in the pan, add the orange juice/spice mixture and stir to mix thoroughly.

Continue to cook an additional 2-3 minutes, stirring almost continuously, until the mixture becomes pasty again.

Stir in the vinegar and lime juice. Simmer 2-3 minutes, until the bananas appear fully cooked, and then remove from heat.

Puree the mixture with a blender or food processor and adjust flavor as needed with salt, lime, or sugar depending on your preferences. Be careful, it is HOT!

Some people like to add food coloring. If so, use 1 or 2 drops each of yellow and red.

Serve at room temperature or chilled.

Yield: about 1-1/2 cups to 2, depending on the bananas

Banana-Rum Ketchup

My daughter provided this recipe and it's a favorite here at the ranch. The little bit of tomato in the sauce doesn't overpower the banana. We serve this with pork chops, fried chicken, or sweet potatoe fries.

Ingredients:

4 large bananas, ripe
1/3 cup sweet onions
3 cloves garlic
1/2 cup golden raisins
1/3 cup tomato paste
1-1/3 cup cider vinegar
3 to 4 cups water
1/2 cup brown sugar
1-1/2 teaspoon salt
1/2 teaspoon ground chipotle chili pepper (or to taste)

1/4 cup light corn syrup
2 teaspoon ground allspice
1 teaspoon ground cinnamon
1/2 teaspoon nutmeg
1/4 teaspoon ground cloves
2 teaspoon dark rum

Preparation:

Peel and chop the bananas. Chop the onions. Chop and crush the garlic.

In a large, non-reactive pot, combine the bananas, onions, garlic, raisins, tomato paste, vinegar, 3 cups water, brown sugar, salt, and ground chipotle chili pepper.

Bring mixture to a boil and then simmer until the ingredients are tender, about 15 minutes, stirring occasionally to prevent sticking.

Working in batches, carefully puree the mixture in a blender, food processor, or with an emersion blender.

If using a blender:
Don't overfill the blender. Be careful when you are processing the sauce in a blender because the hot steam can sometimes blow the lid off. (Guess how we figured that out!)

Start the blender on a low speed with the lid slightly open on one side to vent any steam, then gradually seal the lid and increase the blending speed.

Rinse the pot (or use a fresh pot) and refill with the puree. Bring the ketchup to a boil over a medium-high heat, stirring often. Reduce the heat to low and cook uncovered, stirring the ketchup occasionally, for 1 hour. If the mixture gets too thick and begins to stick, add some of the remaining water (up to 1 cup).

Add the corn syrup, allspice, cinnamon, nutmeg, and cloves. Cook over medium-low heat, stirring often, for another 15 minutes or until it is thick enough to coat a metal spoon. Stir in the rum and remove from heat.

Serve at room temperature or chilled. Store in fridge in covered container for up to two weeks .

Yield: about 3-1/2 cups

Blueberry Ketchup

This sweet berry ketchup is great on grilled burgers and salmon. Adding more chili pepper deepens the flavors.

This recipe calls for 'canning' the sauce to preserve it, so be sure to see the **Notes About Canning** at the end of the book.

Ingredients:

2 tablespoons vegetable oil
1 large clove garlic
1 medium purple onion

2 pints blueberries
1 cup fresh tomatoes (2 medium sized)
2 large purple plums

1/4 cup dark brown sugar, firmly packed
1 tablespoon red wine vinegar
1 large lemon (for zest and juice)
1 medium dried chili pepper
1 tablespoon ginger
1 teaspoon ground cinnamon
1 teaspoon ground cardamom
1 teaspoon ground coriander
1 teaspoon salt
1/4 teaspoon freshly ground pepper

Preparation:

Chop and crush garlic. Finely chop purple onion.

Thoroughly wash the blueberries, discarding any with significant blemishes.

Wash the tomatoes and plums. Quarter and remove the stem ends, tough cores, and any significant blemishes on the tomatoes. De-seed and chop the plums.

Zest the entire lemon. Extract 1 tablespoon of juice.

Heat the oil in a large saucepan (two quart or larger). Add the onion. Stirring often, cook until soft and transparent. Right before the onions are ready, add the garlic.

Add the remainder of the ingredients, stirring well. Cook over medium heat until the mixture begins to simmer. Reduce the heat and keep simmering gently for 30 minutes.

Carefully puree the mixture in a blender, food processor, or with an emersion blender.

If using a blender:
Don't overfill the blender. Be careful when you are processing the sauce in a blender because the hot steam can sometimes blow the lid off. (Guess how we figured that out!)

Start the blender on a low speed with the lid slightly open on one side to vent any steam, then gradually seal the lid and increase the blending speed.

Transfer mixture to a sieve placed over a glass or stainless steel bowl and press with the back of a spoon to extract all the liquid and pulp. You can also do this in a food mill.

Return the puree to a clean pot and heat, bringing the mixture to a simmer. Stirring frequently, cook until thick, about 1 hour.

Pour/ladle hot ketchup into clean, hot jars, (a wide-mouthed funnel is very helpful) leaving 1/2 inch headspace. Wipe rim of jar. Seal with new, pre-simmered lids, and screw down rings firmly.

For pint jars, process:

15 minutes at 0-1000 ft.
20 minutes at 1001- 6000 ft. and
25 minutes above 6000 ft.

Use 5 minutes less for half pints.

Yield: About 3 cups

Cherry Ketchup

This is mouth-watering ketchup has no tomatoes. It is a fruity concoction that is delicious with turkey burgers.

This recipe calls for 'canning' the sauce to preserve it, so be sure to see the **Notes About Canning** at the end of the book.

Ingredients:

2 pounds sweet cherries
1 Ancho chili pepper
1 cup red wine vinegar
2 tablespoons grape juice
1 cup brown sugar
1/4 teaspoon ground mace
1/4 teaspoon salt
1 teaspoon whole mustard seeds
½ teaspoon black pepper
1 teaspoon allspice
1 teaspoon nutmeg

Preparation:

Wash the cherries, and then remove pits and stems. De-stem and de-seed, and finely chop the Ancho chili.

Place cherries, peppers, and all of the other ingredients in a large, non-reactive stockpot. Bring to a boil over high heat, reduce heat, and simmer 10 to 15 minutes, until cherries have softened.

Carefully puree the mixture in a blender, food processor, or with an emersion blender.

If using a blender:
Don't overfill. Be careful when you are processing the sauce in a blender because the hot steam can sometimes blow the lid off. (Guess how we figured that out!)

Start the blender on a low speed with the lid slightly open on one side to vent any steam, then gradually seal the lid and increase the blending speed.

Transfer mixture to a sieve placed over a glass or stainless steel bowl and press with the back of a spoon to extract all the liquid and pulp. You can also do this in a food mill.

Return the puree to a clean pot and heat, bringing the mixture to a simmer. Stirring frequently, cook until thick, about 1 to 1 1/2 hours.

Pour/ladle hot ketchup into clean, hot jars, (a wide-mouthed funnel is very helpful) leaving 1/2 inch headspace. Wipe rim of jar. Seal with new, pre-simmered lids, and screw down rings firmly.

For pint jars, process:

15 minutes at 0-1000 ft.
20 minutes at 1001- 6000 ft. and
25 minutes above 6000 ft.

Use 5 minutes less for half pints.

Store in a cool, dry place until ready to use. Best if left to stand 2 weeks before using.

If you do not wish to can the ketchup, store in a sealed container in the refrigerator up to 3 weeks.

Yield: about 3 half-pints

Cranberry Ketchup

This ketchup is a great with turkey and Cornish Game hens. We don't see fresh cranberries in Texas very often, so we usually only make this around the Fall holidays.

This recipe calls for 'canning' the sauce to preserve it, so be sure to see the **Notes About Canning** at the end of the book.

Ingredients:

2 pounds cranberries
1 cup white or purple onions, finely chopped

1 teaspoon celery seeds
1 teaspoon mustard seeds
1 teaspoon whole allspice
1 stick cinnamon, broken into pieces
1/2 teaspoon peppercorns
2 bay leaves
1 tablespoon salt
1 cup cider vinegar

2 cups brown sugar

Preparation:

Begin by washing the produce. Discard any berries with significant blemishes.

Mix cranberries, onions, and 1 cup water in a large non-reactive pot. Bring to a boil, then cover and simmer 20 to 30 minutes until the berries are mushy, stirring occasionally to prevent sticking.

Carefully puree the berries in a blender, food processor or with an emersion blender.

If using a blender:
Don't overfill the blender. Be careful when you are processing the sauce in a blender because the hot steam can sometimes blow the lid

off. (Guess how we figured that out!)

Start the blender on a low speed with the lid slightly open on one side to vent any steam, then gradually seal the lid and increase the blending speed.

Working in batches, transfer mixture to a sieve placed over a glass or stainless steel bowl and press with the back of a spoon to extract all the liquid and pulp. You can also do this in a food mill. You are trying to process as much of the essence of the fruit as possible.

Rinse the pot (or use a fresh pot) and refill with the strained berry puree. Bring to boil, and cook uncovered until volume is reduced by half. Stir occasionally to prevent sticking.

Meanwhile, in saucepan combine: celery seeds, mustard seeds, allspice, cinnamon, peppercorns, bay leaves, salt, and vinegar. Bring the mixture to a boil. Reduce heat, cover, and simmer for 30 minutes, stirring occasionally. Remove from heat. Let stand while berry sauce is reducing.

When berry sauce is reduced by half, strain the spices and vinegar mixture into the berry sauce. Discard the coarse spice remnants that were strained out.

Add sugar to the sauce, stirring in thoroughly. Cook at a slow boil, uncovered, until very thick. Stir frequently to prevent sticking. Toward the end, you will need to stir the sauce constantly to keep it from scorching.

Pour/ladle hot ketchup into hot jars, (a wide-mouthed funnel is very helpful) leaving 1/2 inch headspace. Wipe rim of jar. Seal with new, pre-simmered lids, and screw down rings firmly.

For pint jars, process:

15 minutes at 0-1000 ft.
20 minutes at 1001- 6000 ft. and
25 minutes above 6000 ft.

Use 5 minutes less for half pints.

Yield: about 2 pints

Fruit Ketchup

My sister-in-law brought this recipe back from Canada, don't 'cha know.

The kids eat it with chicken nuggets, but it goes good with just about any chicken or pork dish.

Getting the fruit ready to process takes some time, so when I make fruit ketchup, I usually double the recipe. Canned properly, it will keep for years.

This recipe calls for 'canning' the sauce to preserve it, so be sure to see the **Notes About Canning** at the end of the book.

Ingredients:

4 cups tomatoes chopped, cored, peeled
4 cups peaches chopped, pitted, peeled
2 cups apples chopped, cored, peeled
1 cup finely chopped onion
3 cloves garlic, finely chopped

1 cup liquid honey
1/2 cup apple cider vinegar
2 teaspoon dry mustard
1 teaspoon salt
1 teaspoon freshly ground black pepper
1/2 teaspoon ground allspice
1/2 teaspoon ginger
1/2 teaspoon celery seed
1/4 teaspoon cayenne pepper

Preparation:

Begin by washing the produce.

If you do not have a food mill/ strainer/sieve, you will need to peel the tomatoes and peaches.

The easiest way to peel tomatoes and peaches is to dip them, a few at a time, into boiling water for a minute or two. Use a ladle to retrieve them, and then plunge them into icy cold water. The skin will slip off with a little help from a knife. (Be careful, they are hot!)

Quarter and remove the stem ends, tough cores, and any significant blemishes on the tomatoes and seeds from the peaches. Place in a large stockpot. Using an old-fashioned potato masher, mash the fruits together until the mixture is a juicy.

Peel, core, quarter, and remove any significant blemishes on the apples, then chop coarsely. Add to the tomatoes and peaches

Coarsely chop the onions, and chop and crush the garlic. Add to the pot as well.

Start the pot over a low heat. Cover the pot and increase the heat until the pot is at a boil, stirring occasionally to prevent sticking. Reduce heat slightly and simmer until the onions are transparent (about 10 minutes). The apples should be very tender as well.

Working in batches, puree the fruit mixture in a blender, food processor, or with an emersion blender.

If using a blender:
You won't be able to do all of the sauce at once, so don't overfill the blender. Be careful when you are processing the sauce in a blender because the hot steam can sometimes blow the lid off. (Guess how we figured that out!)

Start the blender on a low speed with the lid slightly open on one side to vent any steam, then gradually seal the lid and increase the blending speed.

Transfer the sauce to a sieve or colander placed over a glass or stainless steel bowl and press with the back of a spoon to extract all of the liquid. You can also do this in a food mill. You are trying to process as much of the essence of the fruit as possible, leaving behind only a dry-ish pulp.

Rinse the pot (or use a fresh pot) and refill with the strained puree. Add the remainder of the ingredients (sugar, vinegar, and spices).

Bring to a boil over high heat, stirring occasionally. Reduce heat and boil gently, uncovered and stirring occasionally, until mixture is almost the consistency of commercial ketchup, about 45 minutes.

Pour/ladle hot ketchup into hot jars, (a wide-mouthed funnel is very helpful) leaving 1/2 inch headspace. Wipe rim of jar. Seal with new, pre-simmered lids, and screw down rings firmly.

For pint jars, process:

15 minutes at 0-1000 ft.
20 minutes at 1001- 6000 ft. and
25 minutes above 6000 ft.

Use 5 minutes less for half pints.

Yield: about 5-6 pints, depending upon your fruit

Dink's image graces the label of every product that we make because he embodies the spirit of PJR.

His philosophy:
'Eat well, love freely, and stand on top of the car if you can get away with it...'

Grape Ketchup

This is an old recipe that I got from a friend who lived up north. She says that they used to eat it with meatloaf, but we prefer it with lamb. It gives a sweet and sour touch to strongly flavored proteins.

I tried using grape juice instead of whole grapes, and while it tastes the same, it doesn't thicken (I guess it's the pectin in the skins). Most of the time, I don't even strain the skins out, but just cook them in.

Don't expect a light colored sauce. Even when using yellow grapes you will end up with a warm brown color due to the spices.

This recipe calls for 'canning' the sauce to preserve it, so be sure to see the **Notes About Canning** at the end of the book.

Ingredients:

4 pounds ripe concord grapes (or sweet yellow grapes)
2 cups water

1 cup cider vinegar (or red wine vinegar)
2-2 1/2 cups sugar (to taste)*
1 teaspoons allspice
1 teaspoons ground cinnamon, and
1 teaspoons ground cloves,
1 teaspoons salt
1 teaspoons black pepper

Preparation:

* The amount of sugar needed will depend on the sweetness of the grapes.

Begin by washing your produce. Drain. Remove grapes from stems and discard any grapes with significant blemishes.

Place the grapes in a large, non-reactive stockpot. Add water and cook until the grapes are a tender pulp, at least 30 minutes. Mash them as they cook to release juices (I use an old fashioned potato masher).

Stir frequently to prevent sticking. Do not undercook or you will not extract the pectin from the skins and your ketchup will not thicken.

Working in batches, transfer mixture to a sieve placed over a glass or stainless steel bowl and press with the back of a spoon to extract all the liquid and pulp. You can also do this in a food mill. You are trying to process as much of the essence of the fruit as possible.

Rinse the pot (or use a fresh pot) to make sure you've gotten rid of all the skins and refill with the strained grape pulp.

Add the the remainder of the ingredients, and bring to a boil. Reduce heat and simmer uncovered for at least 30 minutes (until there is no free liquid to separate from the pulp).

Pour/ladle hot ketchup into clean, hot jars, (a wide-mouthed funnel is very helpful) leaving 1/2 inch headspace. Wipe rim of jar. Seal with new, pre-simmered lids, and screw down rings firmly.

For pint jars, process:

15 minutes at 0-1000 ft.
20 minutes at 1001- 6000 ft. and
25 minutes above 6000 ft.

Use 5 minutes less for half pints.

Store in a cool, dry place until ready to use. Best if left to stand 2 weeks before using.

Yield: 3-4 pints

Mango Banana Ketchup

Taking only a few minutes to make, this ketchup combines the sweetness of mangos and bananas with a nice spiciness. Like most fruity ketchups, it is best with grilled pork and chicken.

Ingredients:

2 mangos
1 banana, ripe
1/2 of a purple onion
1 clove garlic, chopped
1 tablespoon tomato paste
1 teaspoon sea salt
2 tablespoons light brown sugar, packed
1 tablespoon molasses
1/4 cup apple cider vinegar
1 tablespoon Worcestershire sauce

1/2 teaspoon ground chipotle pepper
3/4 teaspoon ground allspice
1/4 teaspoon nutmeg
1/4 teaspoon ground ginger
1/4 teaspoon ground cloves
1 teaspoon ground cinnamon
1/4 cup orange juice
1/4 cup water

Preparation:

De-seed and peel the mangos, then chop coarsely. Peel and chop the banana. Finely chop the onion. Chop and crush the garlic. Combine with tomato paste, salt, sugar, molasses, vinegar, and Worcestershire sauce.

Puree the mixture in a blender, food processor, or with an emersion blender.

Pour puree into a saucepan. Add ground chipotle pepper, allspice, nutmeg, ginger, cloves, cinnamon, orange juice, and water. Stir thoroughly, and bring to a boil.

Reduce heat and simmer, stirring often, for 10-15 minutes, until ketchup reaches desired consistency.

Serve at room temperature or chilled. Store in fridge in covered container for up to two weeks .

Yield: about 2 cups

Orange Carrot Ketchup

This simple ketchup only takes a few minutes to make and is very good on deli style sandwiches! It's not too sweet and not too sour.

I find that making half a batch is about the right amount for us. This is enough for one meal with two people, as well as some to put in the fridge for a late-night snack.

Ingredients:

1 lb. carrots*
1 Tablespoon butter
1 orange, juiced

1/4 cup orange marmalade
1 teaspoon curry powder
1/2 teaspoon cinnamon
2 tablespoons brown sugar
2 tablespoons apple cider vinegar
Salt

Preparation:

*I've been known to use frozen carrots in a pinch.

Peel and coarsely chop the carrots into rounds. Juice the orange. (don't be concerned if you get some pulp in the juice.)

In a large sauce pan, sauté the carrots in the butter and orange juice until they are tender, about 20-30 minutes, stirring frequently to prevent sticking.

Carefully puree the orange juice and carrots in a blender, food processor, or with an emersion blender.

If using a blender:
Be careful when you are processing the sauce in a blender because hot steam can sometimes blow the lid off. (Guess how we figured that out!)

Start the blender on a low speed with the lid slightly open on one side to vent any steam, then gradually seal the lid and increase the blending speed.

Rinse the pot (or use a fresh pot) and refill with the carrot puree. Add the marmalade, curry powder, sugar and vinegar. Salt to taste. Simmer over low heat, stirring frequently to prevent sticking, until sauce reaches desired consistency, about 30 minutes.

Store in the fridge in a covered container for up to one week.

Peach Ketchup

Like most sweet ketchups, this is particularly good with pork, especially ham. I often make this in the winter, using peaches from our trees that I've frozen or canned during the summer.

This recipe calls for 'canning' the sauce to preserve it, so be sure to see the **Notes About Canning** at the end of the book.

Ingredients:

5 pounds ripe peaches
1 teaspoon of vanilla extract
2 (2-inch) strips orange zest
1 teaspoon mustard seeds
1 cinnamon stick, broken
1 1/2 tablespoon of ground ginger
6 whole cloves
6 whole allspice berries
1 teaspoon nutmeg
2 1/2 cups white wine vinegar (minimum 5% acidity)
2 1/4 cups packed brown sugar
1 teaspoon salt

Preparation:

Peel, pit and quarter the peaches. Remove any significant blemishes and chop coarsely.

Place the peaches in a large, non-reactive stockpot. Add the remainder of the ingredients to the pot and bring to a boil over high heat. Reduce heat to medium, cover, and simmer about 30 minutes, until peaches are extremely soft.

Carefully puree the peach mixture in a blender, food processor, or with an emersion blender.

If using a blender:
Don't overfill the blender. Be careful when you are processing in a blender because hot steam can sometimes blow the lid off. (Guess how we figured that out!)

Start the blender on a low speed with the lid slightly open on one side to vent any steam, then gradually seal the lid and increase the blending speed.

Working in batches, transfer mixture to a sieve placed over a glass or stainless steel bowl and press with the back of a spoon to extract all the liquid and pulp. You can also do this in a food mill.You are trying to process as much of the essence of the fruit as possible, leaving behind only a dry-ish pulp.

Return the peach puree to a clean pot. Bring to boil, and cook uncovered until volume is reduced by half. Stir occasionally to prevent sticking.

When the ketchup reaches the desired consistency, pour/ladle hot ketchup into hot jars, (a wide-mouthed funnel is very helpful) leaving 1/2 inch headspace. Wipe rim of jar. Seal with new, pre-simmered lids, and screw down rings firmly.

For pint jars, process:

15 minutes at 0-1000 ft.
20 minutes at 1001- 6000 ft. and
25 minutes above 6000 ft.

Use 5 minutes less for half pints.

This will also keep in the fridge for about 3 weeks.

Yield: 5-6 pints

Plum Ketchup

Used as sweet and sour sauce for burgers around the Pickle Jar Ranch, this sauce is a staple in our pantry because we have plum trees.

This recipe calls for 'canning' the sauce to preserve it, so be sure to see the **Notes About Canning** at the end of the book.

Ingredients:

2-1/2 lb. plums, pitted

1 cups cider (or red wine) vinegar
1/2 tablespoon cinnamon
1/2 tablespoon allspice
1/2 teaspoon cloves
1/2 teaspoon salt
1/2 teaspoon black pepper

1-1/2 or more cups of brown sugar*

* The amount of sugar needed will depend upon how tart the plums are. I typically start with 1-1/2 or 2 cups, and add only as much as the ketchup needs. Tart wild plums will require significantly more sweetening than a sweet hybrid plum.

Preparation:

Begin by washing the produce. Discard any that are spoiled or damaged.

Place the plums in a large, non-reactive stockpot. Add enough water to just cover the plums. Bring to a boil, then cover and simmer 20 to 30 minutes, until the plums are mushy, stirring occasionally to prevent sticking.

While the plums are cooking, combine the remainder of the ingredients, except the sugar, in saucepan. Bring the mixture to a boil. Reduce heat, cover, and simmer for 30 minutes, stirring occasionally. Remove from heat. Let stand until needed.

When the plums are tender, strain the plums out of the water. I keep a cup or two of the water just in case I need to use it to thin the ketchup, but discard the rest.

Working in batches, transfer mixture to a sieve placed over a glass or stainless steel bowl and press with the back of a spoon to extract all the liquid and pulp. You are trying to extract as much of the essence of the plum as possible, leaving behind only a dry-ish pulp of skin and seeds.

Rinse the pot (or use a fresh pot) to make sure you've gotten rid of all the skins, and refill with the strained plum pulp.

Strain the spices and vinegar mixture into the berry sauce. Discard the spice remnants that were strained out.

Bring to a boil, then reduce to a simmer. Gradually add the sugar, stirring thoroughly with each addition, until sweet to taste.

Simmer about 1 hour, uncovered, until thickened. Stir frequently to prevent sticking.

When the ketchup reaches the desired consistency, pour/ladle hot ketchup into hot jars, (a wide-mouthed funnel is very helpful) leaving 1/2 inch headspace. Wipe rim of jar. Seal with new, pre-simmered lids, and screw down rings firmly.

For pint jars, process:

15 minutes at 0-1000 ft.
20 minutes at 1001- 6000 ft. and
25 minutes above 6000 ft.

Use 5 minutes less for half pints.

Yield: 2-3 pints

Notes

You can never tell exactly how much a recipe will make because while two pieces of fruit may appear identical, one will have less water in it than the other. When you are cooking the ketchup down, you are removing water. So be prepared and have a few extra jars ready.

As a rule of thumb, I presume that each medium sized tomato weighs about 1/4 of a pound (4 ounces). When a recipe calls for 6 pounds of tomatoes, I go get 24 or so medium to large tomatoes, depending on what's in the garden. (That's a lot of tomatoes!)

While fresh garden tomatoes are always my first choice, if I don't have fresh tomatoes available from my garden I will sometimes use canned tomatoes. You can substitute canned crushed tomatoes for some, or all, of the fresh tomatoes in these ketchups, although it will affect the flavor somewhat. If you chose to use canned tomatoes, in tomatoes as in most products, you get what you pay for. So don't go for the cheapest. You will end up with a lot of tough cores and water. Also, read the label and make sure there are no added salts, spices, or preservatives.

When substituting canned tomatoes for fresh, it can get confusing because the same term, ounces, is used to measure weight and volume. There are 16 ounces in a pound (weight) and 8 ounces in a cup (volume). But a cup doesn't necessarily weigh a half pound. Think of a cup of feathers and a cup of lead...

I work under the assumption that 1 cup of chopped tomatoes weighs 6 ½ ounces. After doing some quick calculations, I came up with some basic guidelines.

When substituting canned crushed tomatoes for fresh, I figure that:

- One 28 oz. can of crushed tomatoes is roughly equal to 1-1/2 pounds of fresh tomatoes (or five medium to large tomatoes)
- One gallon of canned crushed tomatoes will equate to about 6-1/2 pounds of fresh tomatoes.

And about the amount of sugar in the ketchup... some people like their ketchup sweeter and some fruit is naturally sweeter; all of the quantities of sweeteners that I recommend are averages and based upon my family's tastes. Feel free to adjust *anything* in the recipe.

About Canning

Do not be intimidated by the term "canning". The jelly that you ate with breakfast this morning was canned. As are all the jarred foodstuffs that fill the grocery store shelves.

Canning is a reliable and safe way of preserving food. It is also easy to learn.

Foods that are high in acid are the easiest to can. And when you add vinegar or citrus juice to a food, you are increasing its' acidity. That's why ketchup is so easy to make and process.

If I am not sure if particular ketchup has enough acid in it to successful can, I refrigerate it. That's why some of my recipes do not include canning instructions.

Fruit Jars

We ordinarily package our ketchup in pint-sized 'fruit jars' because we are a large family. We have been known to eat an entire jar of ketchup at a single meal. (They are called 'fruit jars' because they are most often used to can and store fruit.)

We typically gift in 1/2 pint 'jelly' jars. We also use ½ pints for some of our more exotic or robust ketchups.

When you buy fruit jars, they generally come with 'rings and lids'. The 'ring' part is a metal bracelet with threads. The 'lid' part is a flat disc with a ring of rubber on the underside. When the ring is tightened down onto the threads of the jar, the rubber ring on the lid creates a seal.

This two-part system is particularly handy because the next time you want to can you can reuse your jars and rings, and will only buy have to new lids. Always use new lids when canning.

A bit of fruit-jar etiquette: if you are given a jar of home-made jelly or produce, it is considered bad manners to not return the empty jar.

I can purchase fruit jars at most grocery and hardware stores in Texas. I'm not sure where you would go if you lived in New York City… maybe Wal-Mart.

Canning

An important thing to know about fruit jars is that while they can handle *extreme* temperatures, they can't handle *abrupt* temperature changes. So don't pour boiling ketchup into a room temperature jar. (And don't put a hot jar directly on a cold, stone countertop either!)

You should also wash your jars before using them, even if they look clean. I prepare my jars by washing them in the dishwasher right before I am going to use them. If my timing is right, I can leave them in the dishwasher where they are nice and warm until I need them. This seldom happens…

So I heat usually my jars while my sauce is simmering and cooking down. I put the open jars in a deep pot and cover them with water. The pot I intend to use for 'processing' works well for this. I slowly heat the water and hold the jars at a simmer.

I also bring the lids to a boil, and hold them simmering in a sauce pan. The manufacturer will specify how long they need to simmer in order to properly soften the rubber ring that seals the jar. It will be on the box, but usually it's just a minute or two.

When my sauce is cooked down, and my jars are heated up, I take a large dish towel and fold it in half on the counter next to the stove. I place my largest square cake pan on it.

I dip two or three cups of water out of the pot that holds the simmering jars and pour it into the square cake pan. I pull the jars out of the boiling water, drain them, and sit them in the water in the square cake pan. The cake pan holds enough hot water to keep the jars warm, keeps them from directly touching my counter top, and catches any spills that occur while filling the jars. The dishtowel under the pan protects my marble counter top from the heat.

(Leave the heat going under the water in the pot; you are going to use it again in a few minutes.)

Now you are ready to fill the jars.

Using a ladle (and a canning funnel if you have one), fill the jars with ketchup to the point where the neck joins the body of the jar, 1/2 an inch from the top. When canning, you are creating a vacuum in the jar and this is the amount of 'head room' that you need.

After the jars are filled, use a clean cloth to wipe the top rim of the jar, removing any sauce on the lip of the jar so that the rubber ring on the lid can make a good seal.

Place a lid on top of the jar, rubber side down, and turn a ring down on it. Using a hot pad or heavy dishcloth to hold the jar, carefully tighten the ring down firmly.

Gently place the filled jars in the simmering stockpot of water. Be careful!

In order to process the ketchup, the jars should be covered by at least an inch of water. If adding the jars tries to make the pot to overfill, just dip water out with a ladle. If the jars are not adequately covered, slowly add hot tap water until the jars are adequately covered.

Bring the water to a boil, and cook the jarred ketchup for the prescribed length of time. Timing begins when the water comes to a boil. (This boiling time is called "processing").

Because air is thinner at higher elevations, the elevation of the geographic location of where you are canning effects how long the ketchup should be processed.

For pint jars, I use:

15 minutes at 0-1000 ft.
20 minutes at 1001- 6000 ft. and
25 minutes above 6000 ft.

And use 5 minutes less for half pints.

You will often see a fine stream of bubbles come out of the jars as they are processing. This is normal. In fact, it's good.

After the ketchup has processed for the prescribed amount of time, carefully remove the jars from the boiling water, and place on a folded dishtowel to allow the jars to cool.

As the jars cool, you will hear a distinct 'ping' from each jar. This is the sound of the lid sealing and indicates that a proper vacuum was achieved.

After the sauce has cooled, if you aren't sure whether a jar sealed, you can push down on the center of the lid.

- If the lid does not push down, it is sealed.
- If the lid pushes down and stays down, it is sealed.
- If the lid pushes down and pops back up, the jar is not sealed.

Unsealed jars should be refrigerated and treated as an open, fresh product. Meaning that it's good to eat, but refrigerate it...

After they have cooled, mark the date and type of ketchup on the lids of your jars with a marker. I do this even when I will be putting a label on my jars.

Pots & Pans and Stuff

If I were making a list (which I am) I'd say that you are going to need these basic tools:

8-10 quart pot(s)
Any time you are cooking or working with tomatoes and high acid fruits, you should use "non-reactive" vessels. This means that your pots should be stainless steel or enamel coated. Not aluminum or cast iron. Thick bottom pots work better because they heat more evenly and the fruit is less likely to stick. But if you are willing to stir, you can make thinner bottomed pots work.

If you intend to 'can' any of the ketchups on this cookbook, your 'processing' pot needs to be at least 2 inches taller than your ketchup jars. For pint jars, you really need a container at least 10 inches deep.

I have found that the most versatile pots are tall, stainless steel, pasta pots. Although I could get by with only one, I have two. It makes things a lot easier if I don't have to wash ketchup out of the pot before I can process the jars.

Sauce pan
You will need a small sauce pan, at least 2 quarts. Like the stock pot, the saucepan needs to be non-reactive, because you will be using it to heat vinegar and spices.

Knives
You will need a small paring knife and a good chopping knife. Don't use knives with wooden handles. The grain of the wood and the gap between blade and handle is a haven for bacteria. (This is so much an issue that most State Health Departments do not allow wooden handled knives or utensils in commercial kitchens.)

Sharp knives are easier to work with and much safer than dull knives. Spend $10 and buy a knife sharpener. You won't regret it.

Cutting board
Again, keep wood out of the kitchen. Additionally, I keep a separate board for fruits and vegetables.

Glass or stainless steel mixing bowls
Bowls should be non-reactive as well. That means glass or stainless.

Years ago, I spent $15 on a nest of three stainless steel mixing bowls in gradient sizes. (The largest holds 8 quarts.) I have never regretted my purchase. They are light, durable, and easy to clean. You will only have to buy one set in your entire lifetime, although I recently added an extra-large bowl to my basic set.

Glass bowls are great, just be sure that they are "Pyrex" or made of some sort of material that can handle very hot liquids.

Be cautious of crockery. Beneath its' thin glaze, it is filled with tiny pockets/bubbles that can hold moisture and food particles if the glaze is cracked or broken. Cracked, chipped, or de-glazing crockery should be never be used in canning, as it is a breeding ground for bacteria.

Measuring cup and measuring spoons
Again, these need to be glass or stainless. I use an old 2-cup glass 'Fire King' measuring cup every day. It is easy to read and it has a handle. I think it came from a garage sale. One of the great things about the glass measuring cup is that I can put it in the microwave without worrying. I use stainless steel measuring spoons.

Long handled spoons
You need a couple of long handled spoons for all that stirring. And at least one with slots so that you can pick up and strain fruit out of a deep pot. Yes, they need to be non-reactive (stainless steel) as well...

Ladle
Once the ketchup is made, you need to safely transfer it to your jars. A long handled, and need I say 'non-reactive', ladle is a must.

Food mill, food strainer, or coarse sieve/colander
You need some way to strain the miscellaneous pits and pith from the yummy goodness of the ketchup. At the very least, you need a simple colander. A strainer with stainless wire mesh is better. The best is a food mill.

I use an antique 'potato ricer' which looks like a funnel-shaped colander on legs. It came with a wooden pestle to push the pulp through the holes. (I use a silicone spatula.)

Blender
I don't have a food processer, so everything goes through my blender. It isn't a fancy model. It has three speeds and a pulse option. And a glass bowl. It does the job just fine. (I have to admit that I've been looking at immersion blenders...)

Tongs
You need a set of tongs to use when lifting your finished product out of the boiling water. Special tongs, called a 'jar lifters' are available and are very handy.

Canning funnel
While not necessary, it does make filling the jars easier. It is a short wide funnel whose mouth just fits inside the neck of a fruit jar. Mine is silicone and collapsible for storage.

About the Author

After living on fast food and prepackaged fodder for over twenty years, the author might be considered an expert on commercially made ketchup.

She didn't learn to cook despite (or maybe because of) childhood summers in Texas that included long, hot days of canning peaches, tomatoes, and green beans alongside her mother and grandmother.

When she decided that she wanted to have her grandchildren remember trips to her small goat farm as filled with love, laughter, and good food, she had no choice but to buckle down and figure out how to use the stove in the kitchen.

Much to the amusement of her children, her grandchildren seem willing to taste her culinary experimentations when they visit Pickle Jar Ranch.

Questions and/or comments can be sent via email to:
KetchupCook@gmail.com

Printed in Great Britain
by Amazon

38948693R00036